Please return/renew this item by the last due date.
Library items may be renewed by phone on
030 33 33 1234 (24 hours) or via our website

www.cumbria.go

D1464948

Ask for a CLIC password

Kerry Hardie was born in 1951 and grew up in County Down. She now lives in County Kilkenny with her husband, the writer Seán Hardie. Her poems have won many prizes, and she is a member of Aosdána.

She has published five collections with The Gallery Press in Ireland: *A Furious Place* (1996), *Cry for the Hot Belly* (2000), *The Sky Didn't Fall* (2003), *The Silence Came Close* (2006) and *Only This Room* (2009). Her *Selected Poems* was published by The Gallery Press in Ireland and Bloodaxe Books in Britain in 2011. Her first novel, *Hannie Bennet's Winter Marriage* appeared in 2000; her second, *The Bird Woman,* was published in 2006.

Kerry Hardie

SELECTED POEMS

BLOODAXE BOOKS
in association with
GALLERY BOOKS

ISBN: 978 1 85224 890 1

First published 2011 in Britain by
Bloodaxe Books Ltd,
Highgreen,
Tarset,
Northumberland NE48 1RP
and simultaneously in Ireland by
The Gallery Press.

www.bloodaxebooks.com
For further information about Bloodaxe titles
please visit our website or write to
the above address for a catalogue.

Supported by
**ARTS COUNCIL
ENGLAND**

Edited by Peter Fallon and originated at The Gallery Press.

Cover design: Neil Astley & Pamela Robertson-Pearce.

Printed in Great Britain by
Bell & Bain Limited, Glasgow, Scotland.

Contents

for Seán —
for thirty years

We Change the Map

This new map, unrolled, smoothed
seems innocent as the one we have discarded —
impersonal as the clocks in rows
pacing the upper border, showing time zones.

The colours are pale and clear, the contours
crisp, decisive, keeping order.
The new names, lettered firmly, lie quite still
within the boundaries that the wars spill over.

It is the times.

I have been always one for paths myself.
The mole's view. Paths and small roads and the next bend.
Arched trees tunnelling to a coin of light.
No overview, no sense of what lies where.

These days I want to trace and memorize
the shape of every townland in this valley.
Name families, count trees, walls, cattle, gable ends,
smoke-soft and tender in the near blue distance.

Where were we, Who were we,
What was the Journey?

1

The ferry heaves, nudges the land back,
pushes to sea. We turn to each other,
butting our way into storm.

It is like growing
the shiny inside of an oyster shell. Nosing out
whorls and hollows; gorging valleys; flowing over
the smooth places. Later, when the flood tide drops,
the soft-bodied creatures that smell of fishes, of sea,
shrink and retreat. The shells lie out on the sands.

2

Inland in France the flowering grasses
were blowing and bowing themselves. They
were courtiers in watered silks: tawny and rose
with a pale nap stroked to the light
where the wind ran — a king's glance
conferring its arbitrary grace.

'The Fair Fields of France.' That lovely phrase
was in my eyes, over and over. It was green
and worshipful. It was a Book of Hours,
it was the covetous soul of Plantagenet England
honed with longing. I gave it like obeisance,
gave it like heart's tribute, never exacted.

And yet we left them. We left them
for the coasts, the Northern seas, the places
where boats rose on the tide and shells lay.

3

It always pleased him that the word for those
great horned shells from the warm seas was *conch*
meaning cunt. How they wound themselves
into their shining coral-red interiors.

For myself I loved the sea journey.
How in the afternoon we sat by the rails and stared
at the vast, quiet glitter. Sometimes a gannet voyaging
the surface. Sometimes a ship far off by the horizon.

May

for Marian

The blessèd stretch and ease of it —
heart's ease. The hills blue. All the flowering weeds
bursting open. Balm in the air. The birdsong
bouncing back out of the sky. The cattle
lain down in the meadow, forgetting to feed.
The horses swishing their tails.
The yellow flare of furze on the near hill.
And the first cream splatters of blossom
high on the thorns where the day rests longest.

All hardship, hunger, treachery of winter
forgotten.
This unfounded conviction: forgiveness, hope.

Solstice

for Marie Foley

By a sliding river
to gather a quiver of feathers,
night reaching
far into day.

Mud and the gleam
of low light on mud.
Small mud-splashed bullocks
at the empty cattle feeder.

Rook, raven, hooded crow.
In the woods a ruckus
of wings; knave magpie
rattles and rules.

Arrow and flail,
hollow-iron twilight,
the gutting crow,
the fox at the ribs.

Nearer it draws, and nearer.
Feather of raven winging
the striped arrowhead
of our old-bone winter.

On Having to Stay Behind and Mind the Hearth

Sun out, wind up,
all the new chestnut leaves
racing into the morning.
Heart
chases after them.

Gone now. *Over the hills and far away.*
Into the spring, its green veils.

Heart never wants
to bide quiet here in its place again.
It knows something different now:
wilder, fresher, more abiding.

Heart, Heart,
let me go with you.

February Horses

The horses are moving
down through the gap, treading a way
from upper meadow to lower,
past the red barn

crouched in a pattern of branches;
five of them, chestnuts, one with a blaze,
hooves pulling against
the steady suck of mud.

They have been waiting up there
all through the night;
now they straggle
the cropped and boggy pasture.

Nothing can quell the leap of the eye seeing
the long manes in the stripping wind,
the rhythm of bone and muscle under the mudded coats,
the pooled eyes;

and nothing can quell the gravitas of awe that they impart
to the thin, dark morning,
lights burning,
the sediment of long defeat stored in the bone.

The Farm Girl Remembers Home

She spoke of that birthday,
of stories, one on another,
leaf drifting on leaf.
She spoke for a lost life,
for her own heart's yearning
now that she lives
outside the walls.

She spoke as one looking
on night-starry skies
when we are grown leaf-thin, violable,
and the high dreams float about our heads
and press through our waking selves;
her eyes, helpless and rapt,
watching herself dissolve.

What was she, only a country girl
in city trappings,
the gee-gaws in her ears
his fairings given her in some Glasgow bar?
Taking the pins from her crowned head,
letting the hair fall loose,
she could have been anyone's 'Brown Colleen,
the star of the County Down'.

It wasn't a happiness that had been,
and now was lost, in a city full of cries.
Only the bright squared quilts
spread airing in the yard.
The rest was tear-trails
down an ashey childhood.
It was a longing for her place,
to know her task, fend off this loneliness.

Listening, I was that, too;
I wanted to go back behind the walls
where I had lived and never lived,
to be again the peaty loam
and listen, sodden through womb ears,
to ancient dark-brown dreams,
leaf singing unto leaf,
stained water to stained light.

Ship of Death

Watching you, for the first time,
turn to prepare your boat, my mother;
making it clear you have other business now —
the business of your future —
I was washed through with anger.

It was a first survey,
an eye thrown
over sails, oars, timbers,
as many a time I'd seen that practised eye
scan a laden table.

How can you plan going off like this
when we stand at last, close enough, if the wind is right,
to hear what the other is saying?
I never thought you'd do this, turning away,
mid-sentence, your hand testing a rope,

your ear tuned
to the small thunder of the curling wave
on the edge of the great-night sea,
neither regretful nor afraid —
anxious only for the tide.

The Return

When I came back alone to the house
it wasn't the same. Something to do
with not being the object
of anybody's care or scrutiny —
Attentive.
Still.

Like an old house, fallen in,
lilac growing over the empty doorway,
blackthorn at the gable end —
its fruiting of blue-black sloes,
the dense air
caught on its thorns.

And I thought, is that what we are like?
Our own selves,
unregarded?
Do we stand somewhere,
as secret, sufficient, fierce?
And burdened with fragrance, as lilac?

The Hunter Home from the Hill

Quiet by the window of the train
watching the blanched skies, the bleaching stubble,
a breaking down of colour
to something matt and porous and not at the heart of vision —

watching the winter lying down in the fields
as a horse lies — bone following bone —
the long ridge, the sheep, the blue note of the beet fields,

the bungalows on rutted patches starting awake
out of wild dreams in which they are gardens,

Carlow, the ugly here and there of it, the damp-stained houses,
the sky over the beet plant sausaged with fat round smoke,

all as it is,

like watching him in the kitchen in the morning,
his vest, his thinning slept-in hair, the way he is in your life,
and you content that he be there.

Siblings

The Derryman told of the childhood holiday in the village in Donegal and how he had gone with his father and caught a fish and had carried it home through the blue evening; and the pride of it, greeting people and them knowing, and his mother ready at the stove to cook it. How they had eaten the fish and it had lived inside him for years and years, as Jonah lived in the whale, only the other way round, and then when he was grown with a son of his own he went back to the village and there was no river in it or near it or flowing past it, no river at all.

1

There was a fish but no river
there was no river so there was no fish
there *was* a fish whether or not there was a river
and if there was a fish there *must* have been a river —
and anyway there was the blue evening
not to mention his father's hand on his shoulder.

2

We are always there, you and I, at the table
leaning forward, our elbows together
and our feet braced, our hands locked
and our eyes locked, and I do not know
any of the people crowding dimly
around us as we sit, implacable
at the fulcrum of our clasped hands,
ready at any moment
to force down the other's arm.

We argue, my brother, of fishes, of rivers,
yet you have pulled fish and I have pulled fish
thudding onto the bank, heaving, shining,
from the river that was no river.

Red Houses

for Frances

There are in this country, off small roads in darkness,
certain red houses.
Not the red of blood but the red of fire:
red from the red women who live in them.

I have been in one such house.
There was nothing special, nothing to show.
The wooden gates stood open, the dogs were in,
and on the raw concrete step a bicycle

sprawled on its side in the thick black night air
that laid its wet finger to my face. Inside
the dark-haired red woman-of-the-house
stood by the table, pulled all eyes to her, and it was not

what she said, or did, or looked like, but the place
she drew her life from (some old ferned well
whose whereabouts I did not know) which so tuned her
that she glowed the house.

Fear for the children of such women,
especially the sons. For if they miss
the moment when it might be possible
to make the thing over again

they will spend their lives searching
through people and countries
and nowhere will they find again the red house
with the red heart in the soft black rainy night.

Five O'Clock Strand

for Pat Murphy

You sit in the grass, eyes closed, hands wrapped around your
    knees,
playing the game of 'What do I hear', hearing the sunny
    stillness,
the plate moved on the drainer in the house behind,
the two girls on the stones above the sands —
their fidget of shifting stones, their quiet talk, their laughter —
the dog inland — his few barks — the bee strayed from the
    clover.

The five o'clock news — its first unguarded sentence —
the lazy sound of the sea not even trying,
the fizz of the drying wrack, the wash of the silence.
You open your eyes: the fineness, the stillness, the glitter,
the man who walks the child up the grassy road,
the sea-grass, the tide far out, the absence of treachery,

the starlings fanning out across the sands.
It reminds and reminds of life's base sweetness,
of summers past, of summers not yet lived,
all our small lives, how they are given to us, how we accept
    them,
soft bellow of the cow behind the strand,
a time of day for milking and for tea.

Listening to Tolstoy

There is a lump on her left leg.
In the night she lies awake
and thinks about its presence there.
Then she reaches down
and is amazed how small it feels.

She hears the voices on the radio:
'How does one face death, Gerassim?
What does one do?'
'Nothing. It will all be done for you.
Even the fear will be dealt with
one way or another.'

There is a moment then
as after weeks of rain
seeing a stretch of sky
slung between two hills,
rinsed and cold and thinned as winter washing.

Interlude

for my father

My father told me how he dug up war graves,
picking out thigh bones — two per person — more accurate
than skulls which got mislaid and dumped.

I live in a house in a space in the fields.
This time of year we wake to swallows winging round the
    bedroom;
earwigs and woodlice garrison dropped clothes,
mice quarry soap, harvest-spiders occupy all ceilings.

The house is quietly invaded. He puts down peas and beans;
I watch the fragile blossom of the cherry trees,
the distances smudge-blue, the mountains floating;
sniff the green rain, mourn every passing,
greet each shoot until they are so crowded and so many
I cease recording and admit the summer.

Lives. Theirs, ours. Human times are mostly hard.
They will be so again. Some veil, insubstantial
as wound-gauze, separates this from that.

Avatars

Listen, this is the trinity, he said, tramping the wet road
in the thin well-being of a winter morning:
God the curlew, God the eider,
God the cheese-on-toast.
To his right a huddle of small blue mountains
squatted together discussing the recent storm.
To his left the sea washed.

I thought it was whimsical, what he said,
I condemned it as fey.
Then I saw that he meant it; that, unlike me,
he had no quarrel
with himself, could see his own glory
was young enough for faith still in flesh and in being.
He was not attracted by awe

or a high cold cleanness
but imagined a god as intimate
as the trickles of blood and juice that coursed about inside him,
a god he could eat or warm his hands on,
a low god for winter:
belly-weighted, with the unmistakable call
of the bog curlew or the sea-going eider.

Late Spring

The pike is in the meadow by the river.
He makes lunges. You can see his path gouged
upwards into the flatness of the flood.

He hunts frogs.
Frogs that should be
flopping about in the flowers, practising —
their mottled gold, their greenish patches,
the *pulse pulse pulse* of their underthroats
where the life runs too near the light.

Like the pike.
He may drain back to the river with the spate.
Or lie out on the meadow — bird-stripped bones
in dandelions. Small suns open on a wide green flag.

At St Laserian's Cathedral, Old Loughlin

for my brother, Paddy

I have a lean, long-boned spite in me
against my religious lineage, the rites expected of me —
a spite that is satisfied here in this ruining Cathedral
with its frustration of all those aspirations
of churchmen and congregations.
I don't know what this is bred of —
what unknown disappointments, abuses, expectations,
bubbling through the unreflecting blood.

Yet I'm caught by your grin when I tell you
that these forebears of ours were most likely Cromwellians —
Better than Huguenots, you say. Then I know
that you're seeing yourself, sat with some friend,
his name shifted back into Irish some time around the Rising,
blowing about the Celticness of his home twilight.
Then you'll drop that word into your talk; will watch him
start and then smile at you kindly. Accepting, forgiving.

How it eases something in me to see you so ready
to embrace the disgrace and crow from the still-smoking
    dunghill.
I lay my hand flat on the sun that lies on a webwork of lichen
crawled over a tilted slab. We watch the goats cropping,
the celandines blinking. Around us the graveyard
is steep with the dead. We stroll up the road in the sunshine
to seek out the water, the spring of the matter, the reason
for all this arrangement of stone.

It is all railed-in, tidied and tended. The wellspring's shut fast
inside concrete. It runs from a pipe, the grass patch is mown,
clipped evergreens rail it around. Beech twigs lay lace on the
    sky.
There's a small, worn stone cross

on a plinth where a virgin stands. Ancient.
Not as ancient as she. Nor as the tributes that lie
at her chipped plaster hem. The keys and the beads and
    inhalers;
the lipsticks, their juice-coloured flesh

all chalked in the rain. And I think what a furious place
is the heart: so raw and so pure and so shameless.
We both drink the water. I drink with defiance
and you drink without it. No one is watching, but God,
and He doesn't care, except for the heart's intention.
I think how to live, how to take nothing, leave nothing;
that I will live lightly, as you do. Backwards, like this stone
    cross,
thinned and unwritten by centuries of weather.

Old Men, the Maps in their Heads

for Peter and Jim Aylward

The celandines in the grass,
the crows in the empty ash,
its swooping buds on the sky.

In this white time of spring
they walk the roads like men
drowned yet not knowing it.

Watching them seeing
things seen for years:
their meticulous, still attention —

watching them watching
the cross-hatch of roads, the scatter of fields,
as men who will leave them —

I feel to a denser map
than those patterns of lines and names
that cartographers leak onto paper.

Connemara Easter

for Jen and Ron Bain

The things we saw that day:
the wide bog, planted with flags like broad-swords
growing in blue-green ranks where the eye ran;
the seals in the cove, the hare in the uplands,
the turn of an otter's back in the swell of a wave;
the diver out in the bay, how it rolled over
and preened its white belly and you said
In North America it's called a loon, it's on the stamps.
Then we walked on over the dune-sands
studded with shells and slivers of bone
and star-like plants as in a millefleurs tapestry.

What we carried back with us
into the place where stone became thorn hedges,
where the wild cherry stood in the still of the evening,
and the opened boots of cars on the road home
held harrows and lawnmowers and bales of hay;
what we carried back was a secret.
The white strand, the frail colour of the sea moving over it,
the spring day running out, the empty sands,
the otter's clawmarks, leisurely, a rolling trot,
going into the wash, not coming back, leaving
a small deep awe, kin to strewn grave-cloths.

Vitality

'Tell her to use the pool. Swimming will make her stronger.'

All winter I slipped between its blue sheets, I moved
through the lucent space that did not resist me.
The low day lapped at the windows, the blue rectangle
printed itself on my dreams.
No one but me. I saw snow-fade, light-stretch,
sun-quiver on the pool's blue floor.
Got stronger,
grew
lonely.

         ∾

He told me of a market where they went
to buy blue carp at Christmas when they lived in Prague.

He said in Prague there was an outdoor pool,
you lowered yourself down ladders hung with ice,
you slid beneath white steam that hid the stars.
Arthritics liked to swim there,
and people like them, without baths.
The snow lay banked beside the walkways.
It glittered like salt.

         ∾

The yellowed tiles, the knots and veins,
the scabby unwashed forms.
The inky flicker of a blue carp's tail.

I looked out from my life
and it was silk-thin and too easily torn.

She Replies to Carmel's Letter

It was a mild Christmas, the small fine rain kept washing
    over,
so I coated myself in plastics,
walked further than I could manage.
Leave me now, I'd say, and when they had tramped ahead
I'd sit myself down on a stone or the side of a high grass
    ditch,
or anywhere — like a duck in a puddle —
I'd rest a bit, then I would muddle around
the winding boreens that crawled the headland.

Sometimes, waterproofed and not caring,
I'd sit in a road which was really a stream-bed,
being and seeing from down where the hare sees,
sitting in mud and in wetness,
the world rising hummocky round me,
the sudden grass on the skyline,
the fence post, with the earth run from under it,
swinging like a hanged man.

Then I would want to praise
the ease of low wet things, the song of them, like a child's
    low drone,
and praising I'd watch how the water flowing the track
is clear, so I might not see it
but for the scrumpled place where it runs on a scatter of grit,
the flat, swelled place where it slides itself over a stone.
So now, when you write that you labour to strip off the
    layers,
and there might not, under them, be anything at all,

I remember that time, and I wish you had sat there, with me,
your skin fever-hot, the lovely wet coldness of winter mud
on your red, uncovered hands,
knowing it's all in the layers,

the flesh on the bones, the patterns that the bones push
upwards onto the flesh. So, you will see how it is with me,
and that sometimes even sickness is generous
and takes you by the hand and sits you
beside things you would otherwise have passed over.

The Cruellest Month

for Bernadette Kiely

We came round the bent road in the drowned light
of a spring evening
and I saw you, in your dark coat,
your hair dark, your face white, your hands full of lilacs —

You might have been a bride, the way you walked,
your head high, him beside you, but separate,
like a woman coming from the church a hundred years ago,
going home with the man, to begin the life contracted.

It was all lit
from elsewhere: the stormy evening, the white light,
the small squat houses, the river running black
by the stone quays, the chestnuts climbing.

And those lilacs, a mass of them,
spreading out of your hands:
a white one, a mauve one, a white one —
Not casual. Some eye deciding, some hand arranging
the eye's bidding.

All week I'd been on about lilacs,
had stood by a window in the evening looking down
on a lilac in the garden, its few blooms
with the reddish stain of blood behind their purple —

Those famous lines were in my mind, this being the month,
but it wasn't right — his lilacs, not our lilacs.
Our lilacs: out of a green land, some with blood on their
    roots.
And white ones, planted by the Marian grottoes.
And mauve, plebeian, by the ruined gable ends.

These blooms, drawn to your hands
like the thought-forms of flowers;
their fall over your hands, down the dark coat,
their thick scent on the chilly air.

You, by the quay, walking another century,
as though our dramas act and re-enact on the same stage,
so that I saw you,
and a woman that had gone before you,
and lilacs, clustering into your hands from hers.

Fuller's Earth

for Maeve Malley

I saw at last
that you were made from silvery shale;
that if I rubbed you with my finger

flakes might fall,
all shimmery with bright dust;
that you were set

on being less and less substantial,
on trying to change from flesh
and into something blind,

night-flying, differently attuned.
Soft, thickened wings
of taupe, the body

furred in cinnamon,
eyes black and huge as night
which would grow dazzling

till it was as day.

Exiles

1

This is a work of remembrance, the remembrance of lives.
And of times. Of land, water, sky.
Sometimes there are only the names and the lives are lost;
sometimes there are only the lives and the names are lost.
To remember, in a time of forgetting.

I was standing on spread newspapers,
an altar vase locked under my arm,
my hand's warmth misting its yellow brass,
pulling at the flowers in it, stiff and still fresh,
although it was ten days from Christmas —
and Nancy, beside me in the frozen church,
saying she had Irish in her.

They came away in a mass, their stems embedded,
I had to stamp on them to break the ice
to free out ivy that I wanted for the funeral vases.

My mother-in-law was coming in her coffin
to lie in the stone-dark through the Northern night.
And none of us minded that —
not the coldness nor the sweep of the wind —
because she'd always liked outside, all-weather,
and the next day she would move off, we would follow after
to stand while she took the place prepared for her
in the slit earth in the grey bowl of the hills.

Nancy said it was her father that had made her love the
     music.
Her father was half-Irish; his father had been Irish.

She was trying to make me understand
but I was thinking of flowers
and I didn't. *My father was illegitimate.*
The hardness of the old word focused me.
Her grandfather's name — Sheridan — was on the
    Certificate.
He had come here, but she didn't know why.
Then he had gone away again.

No, she answered me, he hadn't let her down.
He would have married her, her people wouldn't have him.
They sent him off. But they kept his child.

Nancy was telling me this, her eyes bright, fresh,
everything direct, her voice lifting, falling with the Northern
    vowels,
her face young, and there was nothing ever that need be
    hidden
or avoided. She was a shepherd's wife, for forty years
they'd kept a farm on the high moors,
had watched the weather build over Scotland,
the rim of light edging the rise of the land,
the clean rain hanging from the pointed grasses.

She hadn't known my mother-in-law to talk to, only by
    sight.
I thought to say to Nancy, she was Irish too,
although she had the accent of an English lady;
I nearly said it but I didn't,
I wanted to leave Nancy with her Irish grandfather
who had come there and gone away again,
whose name had been Sheridan,
who was likely as not a labourer or a drover.

2

At my feet were florist's bunches:
tiger lilies, spray chrysanthemums.
I wanted holly for its shiny darkness,
so I could drown the florist's flowers in it,
so I could take her back to her beginnings,
which was where she had taken herself through the
    Alzheimer's.
I wanted her to lie there in the frozen darkness,
unharrassed by tiger lilies or chrysanthemums.
My husband, her youngest son, went out into the fading
    light
and cut long spears of holly from the churchyard,
and I broke the stems and thrust them
into the mouths of the vases, brassy as cymbals.

And Nancy said to leave the spent flowers and the bits of
    stem
because it was her turn for cleaning and she loved the
    music —
the fiddles and the pipes. I saw him then, her Irish grand-
    father,
his back turned, tramping away,
over those bleak moors which pulse with larks in summer.

3

She died in the deep of winter
when the cattle break out of the empty fields
when the earth has split open in darkness
and the white mist pours its breath into the night.

On her coffin, only the name she took when she was
    married.
Gone, all of her life before that ceremonial crossing,
all her crowded ancestors are shooed away,
no point them to come peering
over the rim of the darkness like so many gargoyles,
they'll get no satisfaction here, nor any welcome.
Nor would she have wanted them in her lucid days,
but after things started colliding and sliding away
the landscape was all changed and changed
and even her husband of sixty years didn't know its
    contours.
None could say where she roamed nor whom she lived
    with.
All we were sure of was it was not us.

4

In Ireland a man must have a home town,
somewhere to leave behind him, somewhere to long to
   return to.
A woman makes her home town in her children.
In them she makes her claim, in them is her belonging.

Shelagh Jacob was her name.
She has gone into the dark with all the rest of them
and it is 'Nobody's funeral, for there is no one to bury.'
Ah, but there is, there's a husk in a box and all us live ones
waiting to bear witness to a womb
that spewed new generations for the dark.

He, leaving his name, losing his child.
She, losing her name, leaving children.
And what she liked and what she didn't like
is only personality. And the live children that she bore
are only issue. Her one dead child
is only suffering. And there is nothing to lose
for it is all already gone.

5

We stand in the frozen grass;
the skeins of geese fly over —
dissolving, reforming,
thinning out like stitches on leather,
bunching close, like strung beads.

6

The flight home was delayed and we waited, bone tired. I thought of Dublin and the long drive home through the softer, darker Irish night; of how in the morning we would wake in our own place with its small blue mountains and its tangled fields, far from this country of moors and high fells and rapid broken streams.

I thought of the man Sheridan, his boots and his stick.

7

And now it is near to the solstice again.
The old man, her husband, is dying.
Slowly. The body, taking its time.
And evening after evening, all through the year
after the urgent work, I have sat with this piece,
trying to understand; failing.
And all I have left is remembrance,
frail and wavering as dream.

This is a work of remembrance, the remembrance of lives.
And of times. Of land, water, sky.
Sometimes there are only the names and the lives are lost,
sometimes there are only the lives and the names are lost.
To remember, in a time of forgetting.
In the long wail of the pipes, the language of remembrance,
and Nancy, her clear eyes looking ahead,
her yearning and remembrance in the music.

Signals

A morning of swift grey skies,
crows walking the wet roads.

Then, just before Carlow,
a field got up and took to the air:
white-bellied birds, their dark, splayed wings
flopping up into the sky.

In the night I had woken
to this new cold, draping my shoulders.
The hand, plunged deeper into the black pool.
Now, here were the lapwings
rising up from the rushy field;
lapwings, flying out of the north,
filling the skies with their old, fierce weather.

And what can we do
but what must be done,
no matter what is lost or left behind us?

And I knew there'd be more flocks on the skyline
when we reached the bleak, wide flatlands of Kildare.

After the Storm

A wind from the south
bowls the summer's last sweetness before it.
Hollyhocks lie out on the wet grass,
their storm-flattened flowers of sodden white crêpe
still budded tight. Already they have lost
themselves.
      The swallows and martins
are blowing all over the sky which has heightened and
    stretched
like Leonardo's man, describing his full circle.
The earth has grown smaller and denser,
the tight packed muscle of the diaphragm
hoarding its power. The trees lift their burdened branches
up into the windy, white sky
like souls that crave nakedness.
        There is an urgency
in the warm wind, a new vigour. Like a man, who,
waking one morning in late middle age,
sees the flowers take on garment of fire,
the smoke hues lick under the brightness.
These sombre washes tightening the world,
thickening its dark honey.

Autumn's Fall

It seems the rain will be its end — the smell
of rotting-down in ditches, under trees,
the sharp scent of late apples in wet grass,
the spent leaves guttering in the stone-flagged well.

The spaces in the branches stretch and grow.
High spiralling of crows in the thin sky.
The grey drift of the distance. Nothing more
of hope or exultation in the flow

of damp air from the windows that I leave
to let the year move quietly through the house
preparing for the long dark and the cold,
loosening the nets spent thoughts still weave,

clingy as cobwebs. There must be space for death,
and witness for this seep of emptying light;
for winter, pressing with the cattle at the gate,
clouding the darkness with their frightened breath.

Northumberland

for Katie

She showed me the frosted tufts
of the winter barley,
the stalks cut square and close
where the geese had grazed.

She showed me a rheumy eye
in the iron meadow,
the growth rings in its ice
like marks in a cut tree.

She said when the hoar frosts came
the hairs on the cattle
stood shining and separate.
The thorns glittered.

The land lay all around
like an opened hand.
The sky leaned down
and laid its face there.

Things that are Lost

My mother teaches me the fading skills:
how to clean fish, plait garlic, draw pheasants;
how to distinguish wading birds,
how to make linen lace.

I know her ache because it is in me.
I try to teach to anyone who'll listen
wild flowers: their legends, properties, names.
I do this in full love of the fresh world.

But a voice says,
Lose things, forget them, let them go.
See all things always the first time.
Unnamed. In wonder.

What's Left

for Peter Hennessy

I used to wait for the flowers,
my pleasure reposed on them.
Now I like plants before they get to the blossom.
Leafy ones — foxgloves, comfrey, delphiniums —
fleshy tiers of strong leaves pushing up
into air grown daily lighter and more sheened
with bright dust like the eyeshadow
that tall young woman in the bookshop wears,
its shimmer and crumble on her white lids.

The washing moves on the line, the sparrows pull
at the heaps of drying weeds that I've left around.
Perhaps this is middle age. Untidy, unfinished,
knowing there'll never be time now to finish,
liking the plants — their strong lives —
not caring about flowers, sitting in weeds
to write things down, look at things,
watching the sway of shirts on the line,
the cloth filtering light.

I know more or less
how to live through my life now.
But I want to know how to live what's left
with my eyes open and my hands open;
I want to stand at the door in the rain
listening, sniffing, gaping.
Fearful and joyous,
like an idiot before God.

That Old Song

Because it is so lovely —
the wind sweeping the poplars,
the cloudy darkness gathering
bluish over the high whitethorn,
their burden of blossom as though sliding
from off their stiff branches
into dim grass.

Us too, our living sliding from us —
creamy, fragrant, and discarded —
so it seems easy to unfetter,
easy to move upwards
in the slow dusk of late May, early June.
And I, thinking: I don't have to remember or hold on,
I live this now, it is deep in the life.

After My Father Died

The sky didn't fall.

It stayed up there,
luminous, tattered with crows,
all through
January's short days,
February's short days.

Now the year
creeps towards March.
Damp days, grass springing.
The poplars' bare branches
are fruited with starlings and thrushes.
The world is the body of God.
And we —
you, me, him, the starlings and thrushes —
we are all buried here,
mouths made of clay,
mouths filled with clay,
we are all buried here, singing.

Rain in April

I was squatting beside Carmel's lilies of the valley,
poking with my finger, loosening the soil,
providing a bit of encouragement
for the wands of white bells they're about to make,
bells with a scent on them thick as a wall,
a scent that would drown you in remembrance,
when suddenly the April wind rose up and dumped
a pouring of silver-grey rain on my back and my head
and I saw him run for the house but I stayed,
liking the cold wetness and the sudden rip
of the wind rocking the birch and sounding
the wooden chimes in the japonica,
a tree that is being daily denuded
of its rose-red buds by the bullfinches that we watch
as we sit in bed drinking morning tea and marvelling
at their crunch and spill of tender bud all around,
then speak of the sense in shooting them as my grand-
     mother did,
lining their shameless plumage up in the sights
of her single-barrelled shotgun, dropping them
out of as-yet-unstripped apple trees, the same grandmother
who planted my childhood with lilies of the valley.
So I was squatting there, and everything was thin —
thin grass, thin light, thin buds, thin leafing of trees,
thin cloud moving fast over thin smoke-blue of the
     mountain —
and I knew this thinness for promise-to-be-delivered,
lovelier even than May — the promise delivered —
like the thinness of some people who never quite settle here,
never grow solid and fixed in the world,
                              and *Yes*, I was thinking,
April is like this, some people are like this, in a minute or two
the rain will pass over, the light will fill out,

and this strange thin moment that's see-through to somewhere
  else
will have bowled away off with the rainy wind up the
  valley —

Flow

That morning, the drive through rain down the twisted road.
Wild cherry, its scatter of blossom and leaves, its windy
   spaces.
One swallow dipping ahead, the first you've seen,
you following in the scoop of air between bare hedges.

Then, the white room under the eaves, the fire,
the wind sounding an old sound in the chimney.
The jam jar on the mantelpiece, its few leaves,
its criss-cross of unopened bluebells scoring the wall.
Day-candles: the sound-thread as the wax runs off
in quick stream onto the dark hearthstone.
The opened heart, its fragrance in the undefended light
that pours in white draught through the old, thin windows,
while outside, far below, in long wet grass,
the pheasant's coloured strut, his mating call.

All gone, all yesterday, the bluebells all long over,
dead bees lie out on every shelf and table;
glossed seed-pods wither dry, then harden.
Nothing to hold, no ground beneath the feet,
only the days, their passing. One. Another.

Trapped Swallow

The trees are quiet and moist, they stand
attentive as good children in new clothes,
hands folded before them. I have washed
the blanket and am struggling to heave
its damp mass over the yellow plastic of the line.
It was marked with the swallow's panic,
the swallow I found in the stairwell,
exploding off ceilings and doors;
I caught up with it at last,
scrabbling the window behind a row of pot plants,
closed my hand on its air-light life,
opened a door and threw it up into the sky. My life
is small and I would have it
no other way. The first whitethorn
has broken and martins flicker and skim. Last night,
by the river, I noted the scream of the swifts.
Two grey herons rose up from the bank
and went lumbering into the trees.
Further down, the raven flung
its harsh cry from the woods. It broke
and circled, its blunt wings drubbing the air. A little wind
has come up now, out of nowhere, and with it
a misting of rain. I reverse my heave and pull
at the blanket's felt. With the swallow
suddenly quiet in my hand
I felt the weight of privilege: my dense flesh sheltering
its weightless life. This privilege
crept into my sleep and I woke with it
today. I have this small, deep pain
of understanding nothing. The spring is changing
into summer and I keep adding
years to my life.

Sheep Fair Day

*The real aim is not to see God in all things, it is that God,
through us, should see the things that we see.*
— Simone Weil

I took God with me to the sheep fair. I said, 'Look,
there's Liv, sitting on the wall, waiting;
these are pens, these are sheep,
this is their shit we are walking in, this is their fear.
See that man over there, stepping along the low walls
between pens, eyes always watching,
mouth always talking, he is the auctioneer.
That is wind in the ash trees above, that is sun
splashing us with running light and dark.
Those men by the rails with their faces sealed,
they are buying or selling. Beyond in the ring
where the beasts pour in, huddle and rush,
the hoggets are auctioned in lots.
And that woman — ruddy-faced and home-cut hair,
a new child on her breast — that is how it is
to be woman, milk-running, sitting on wooden boards
with animals and muck and death
as the bidding rises and falls.'

Then I went back outside and found Fintan.
I showed God his hand as he sat on the rails,
how he let it trail down and his fingers played
in the curly back of a ewe. Fintan's a sheep-man,
he's deep into sheep, though it's cattle that earn
him a living.
         'Feel that,' I said,
'feel with my heart the force in that hand
that's twining her wool as he talks.'
Then I went with Fintan and Liv to Refreshments.
I let God sip tea, boiling hot, from a cup,

and I lent God my fingers to feel how they burned
when I tripped on a stone and it slopped.
'This is hurt,' I said, 'there'll be more.'
And the morning wore on and the sun climbed
and God felt how it is when I stand too long,
how the sickness rises, how the muscles burn.

Then later on, at the back end of the afternoon,
I went down to swim in the slide of green river,
working up under the bridge against the current.
Then I showed how it is to turn onto your back
with, above you and a long way up, two gossiping pigeons
and a clump of valerian, holding itself to the sky.
I remarked on the stone arch as I drifted through it,
how it's dappled with sun from the water,
how the bridge hunkers down, crouching low in its tracks
and roars when a lorry drives over.

And later again, in the kitchen,
tired out, at day's ending, and empty,
I showed how it feels
to undo yourself,
to dissolve, and grow age-old, nameless:

woman sweeping a floor, darkness growing.

On Derry's Walls

A thing can be explained only by that which is more subtle than itself; there is nothing subtler than love: by what then can love be explained?
— Sumnûn ibn Hamza al-Muhibb

The blackbird that lives in the graveyard
sits on the Wall at the fade of the winter day.
He has fed off the worms that have fed off the clay
of the Protestant dead.

And yet he is subtle,
subtle and bright
as the love that might explain him
yet may not be explained.

As for the rest, there is almost nothing to add,
not even *This is how it was,*
because all we can ever say
is *This is how it looked to me* —

In the blackbird's looped entrails
everything is resolved.

from *Sunflowers*

for Valentina Gherman-Tazlauanu

LE CHEVAL

The thing I like most about Switzerland —
great unfenced fields of sunflowers
dying in the light.

When we run out of broken-language conversation
we play 'What animal would you be?'
'Un cheval,' she says, quick and soft.

The things I like most about horses —
their strong necks, the planes of their faces,
the way the life sits inside them.

The things I like most about Valentina —
her feminine hands, weight-bearing shoulders,
the way her face lights.

Those sunflowers.
It's not because they are dying —
but I like their bowed heads and that moulded place

where the neck flows into the nape.
Standing so straight, whole armies at prayer
before the last battle is lost.

I DON'T GO TO THE SUNFLOWER FIELD

The rain is falling on the trees and on the vines,
falling on draggled sunflower fields.
It beats on the long windows
that hold such blank and tender rectangles
when they stand open in late August dusk.

ENOUGH

I want to stay in one place for a long time.
I don't care if there aren't any sunflowers.
I want to see the same thing every morning.
I want to rest in the same people.

from *Achill*

ACHILL SEPTEMBER

for Richard Dore

On this island of bones and stones
I catch myself planning
the leaving of gardens.

This urge
to live hunkered into the wind.

On the strand
a new-dead porpoise, then a headless turtle.
A leatherback.
Its big, hinged backbone
working loose from its meat.

The hills
pull free from their moorings,
they drift off under
the vast sky.

Suddenly I'm remembering
the float of sweet peas in Kilkenny dusk.

Apples,
each fruit twisting into the hand.
And wasps,
gorging.

Bones
are gathered here like flowers.

They cut black sods and stack them tight
against the roar of winter.

THE HILL BEHIND THE HOUSE

Each morning here I go to the back window
to check the colour of the sky above the hill.

It is a good hill, small and close and brown,
its loose curve hardly breaking water.

When there is blue behind this arc
it goes on up forever.

When there is thick-and-grey
I know a finite world of bog and sheep,

plain and familiar, a damp sedgy place
that stills the heart till it rests clean and bare.

Autumn

The butterflies are stretched
on the walls and on the sills,
they have spread their wings out quietly to die.

The poplars make their water-sound,
the wooden chimes their *chock-chock* sound;
the turning leaves gleam in the stormy light.

Changing, all things changing,
going down into the darkness,
and the river running shining to the sea.

Winter Heart

Winter again, and I'm glad that the seasons
keep coming around and around.
I am glad that the heart, too, is seasonal,
that it loses its leaves in November,
holds trembling hands to the sky;
that it freezes and thaws and freezes,
running with water in autumn,
singing with birds in the spring.

It is ready again now for darkness
and a night-sky splintered with stars,
for winds, wuthering its stony ramparts,
for fire in the halls within.

When Maura had Died

for Carmel

These days —
           filled with wonder of death.

This morning I woke early,
watched the day come, blue and hard-won,
the rain's clean shine on the glass, the drops
on the crossbar hanging in the light.
I knew dailiness, saw birds
moving across the window, saw the window
for a portal, as in Renaissance painting.

I never knew
that death was this simple;
you left
as a woman holding a letter
moves to the light —

Then I wanted the grace
to share the open secret,
to be wasp in the apple and apple arching
around the devouring wasp,
sheltering its feeding. Oh, let me live living,
devoured and devouring,
eating myself down
to my own core.

Flesh

Sitting in a doorway,
in October sunlight,
eating
peppers, onions, tomatoes,
stale bread sodden with olive oil —

and the air high and clean,
and the red taste of tomatoes,
and the sharp bite of onions,
and the pepper's scarlet crunch —

the body
coming awake again,
thinking,
maybe there's more to life than sickness,
than the body's craving for oblivion,
than the hunger of the spirit to be gone —

and maybe the body belongs in the world,
maybe it knows a thing or two,
maybe it's even possible
it may once more remember

sweetness,
absence of pain.

Flood

Each time I pass there are more swans.
A sedgy field at the best of times.
And the little hills, circling.
And the sag of the sky.

A slow file of cows
treads through a gap in the thorns
under a blaze of white light
that spills through a gap in the sky.

More swans, more water.
The coil of their necks
as they loop and they stretch,
as they puddle the rushy pasture.

Nine today — and the shine
of the low, cold light
on the stretch of the flood —
nine in the wet, mossed grass.

Each time I pass there is more water.
More water, more swans.
And cows, trudging up the green hill.
And the big-bellied sky, great with rain.

Near Loughrea

The lone bull
red on an emerald ground.
The ruined church
through the gap-toothed wall.

Fields
bright with new grass, new lambs.
Sky
gone suddenly spacious and blue.

And the whitethorn breaking.
And the blackthorn making stars.

And one chestnut, standing holy,
its birth-wet buds
held to the high, wide sky.

On Not Visiting My Aunt in Hospital

You'd said, 'I don't want you to go,'
and the strange thing was that I didn't mind
though I ached all over and, outside the window,
the afternoon floated, golden with dust motes;
didn't mind sitting on, talking of this and of that,
answering questions I'd answered ten minutes before.
And afterwards, driving the long drive home,
I'd meant to go back the next day.

But along came the world, rattling and banging my door.
It made such a noise that I turned back the key in the lock.
In barged my life,
hands full of e-mails and faxes and phone-calls,
of things to be said, of tasks to be done,
and, fool that I was, I believed in the force of the world.

Now I'm out of bed once again. I could drive,
but instead I'm here
in the poplars' rustling shade.
The mountains are blue,
the wind's in the trees, the bees
are bumping about in the bells of the flowers.
And I don't want to leave this, I don't want to go there
and wilt in a hospital ward.
Forgive me. A few more days. I just can't make myself
stop the not-wanting of it.
And please do again what you did for me
when you told your friend that I came every day,
and then smiled at me with such sweetness
because you thought it was true.

After Rage

It was only
when I had carried the seedlings
out into the cold day,
when I had sat myself down
in the damp grass
and pricked out
hollyhocks, poppies, lavender, pinks —
the young plants,
the fibrous trail of their webby roots —
firming them
into their new places;
only then
did I quiet enough

for the great winds to die down
in the whitethorns of my being,
for the magpies to leave off their rattling
in the grace of the silver birch.

The High Pyrenees

I lifted my eyes and there was the sea of the mountains,
wave upon wave, and far out on the ocean, white peaks,

then the silence came close and stood there beside me and
   waited,
and I knew there was nothing to want or to fear or to say —

there was only the ancient sea of the mountains,
only the night coming down on the great dark slide of its
   waves.

The Butcher's Wife

for Alex

She was thin
and bony and strong, with eyes
that had wept — you could see that — dark hair
that was greying — too busy for dye —
and patient and quick,
she minced lamb, sliced *serrano*,
sent off the son
to fetch the sheep's cheese — two different kinds —
explained their relative
hardness and softness; her mother
came in from the hall
bearing loops of raw sausage
like bicycle tyres,
went back to the back —
her slippered slap
on the red passage-tiles
before the door closed —
and the butcher's wife
was cutting the cheese,
her apron, washed soft,
had lace at the top and sides of the bib,
it had blood on the linen, blood on the lace,
and Lorca had stuck his head round the door,
still looking for signs
that are ancient and bare,
like blood,
like white linen,
like the loop of her hair, working loose.

The Dregs of the Year

for Colette Bryce

Small birds at the nuts in a frenzy of feeding;
winter
squeezing them
down to the bone.

Old sights, old sounds.
Ceremonial.
Winter,
her ancient ways.

And sheep,
            moving about the wet meadow.
And crows,
            adrift in the faded light.

Starlings.
The rush of their wings.
Bandit bands
whizzing above the drenched land.

Wind rocks the last shrivelled hands
on the chestnut trees.
There's the wedge of a daylight moon
with a bleeding edge

and clouds
blowing over it.

Water. The world. Sodden.

The ash is a rag-tree of crows.

February Snow

The fields are mud.
The first buds on the ash trees
blacken to spear points: stubby, stubbornly raised.

The mountains, ink-blue on their lower slopes,
stand in white silence on a sky
grown passionate with snow-cloud.

Strange visitors,
come to us out of marvellous lands,
proud with a great still pride.

Your China-poem Came in the Post

for Sinéad Morrissey

When I'd finished reading
your poem about your time in China
I wanted to go upstairs
and unpack from some old chest
a length
of saffron-yellow silk.

Silk,
not slithery but stiff,
encrusted with the stuff of being nothing
but itself.
And the enfolding air,
cast off now, but infused, fusty,
with its preciousness
and its yellow being.

I don't know why
this came upon me,
it was something to do
with the unrolled bolt of your journey
and that last part when China
met China in the market place
and they conversed.

You know, the world, when it's smalled down
to what can be seen through two eyes,
is too big and too full of fear,
it cannot be grasped,
it can only be turned into yellow silk
and watched from a kneeling place on the floor,
then
after a long time

touched
        so the touch
yields up a lost domain.

Communication

My father wouldn't talk on the phone.
He gave it to my mother,
then told her what to say to me.
He seemed to need this go-between.
As though without, I was too raw —
the whole complicated business
too risky, too much effort.
My brother is the same,
he phones someone and, if they're in,
he hangs up, rings back later for the answer-phone.

I am less sure —
I think I have to do these things, to prise myself loose
from my nature. Sometimes, after a long call,
I feel betrayed into words
I have not thought through, accused
because I do not want this miracle.
I am too slow to move so fast.

Alone in the house, I let the phone ring for days.
I don't turn on stereo or radio or television.
The membrane of the walls thins like muslin, the light
presses through. Wind sounds, bird sounds,
field sounds of cattle and sheep.
The swish of the crows flowing over.
I live deep in the world
and I grow like my father.

October

All the hillside is blazing
in the hot gold light,
every dying leaf,
blazing —

And the dew-soaked pasture.
And the high sky, sailing with cloud-kites.

And over the ridge, the cirrus wisps
in shining threads of fine, spun hair.

∽

Forgetfulness
up here in the mountains —
my old, slow river, its loved remembrance,
fades like a photograph emptied out by the sun.

In Bed Again

after reading Tu Fu

Five-thirty. February dusk.
The last few tits and finches,
black in the netted branches of the silver birch,
flitter and loop the hanging feeders.
The wheelbarrow lies on its side in the long wet grass,
its yellow handles
rusting into gloom. How tired I am.
But quiet too. Better this
than the exhausted rage that sickness lays
upon my doorstep, as a cat his kill.
How still the garden;
still the rowan and ash. The first lambs
stagger the muddy field. Life passes
slowly, slowly. And all the while
the furious horses gallop
over the endless reaches of the yellow plain.

Solitude

It was January.
I'd hardly seen anyone for days.
The sheep were all sitting separate and silent,
a hard wind was coming in over the hill,
a white moon floated.

I'd bought the pumpkin for soup.
My arms had dropped with the weight of it,
dropped and come back, like the bounce back up into air
after the deep of the river.
I'd hefted it in from the car,
set it down on the table.
It was smaller and fiercer and redder than I'd expected.

I was out on the hill for the sake of the moon
and the ash trees, raking the way with shadow.
Where the road ran high the fields slid into the valley;
cloud covered the slopes of the mountains
laying down snow.
I carried the colour, red fire on the dark of the table,
the colour would bear me through till his return.

When I got home the phone was ringing,
I had the key in the door but it wouldn't turn.
I heard the phone cease in the empty house.
And the dogs milled about.
And the pumpkin stared out at the moon.

Derrynane '05

It was well after seven,
but how could we leave?
It would have been
like spitting in the face of God.
A cormorant surfaced and dived,
surfaced and dived, blue shadows
lay down in the scuffled footprints,
the long, glass waves curled over
and broke into spatters of light.

Yellow rattle, eyebright, bedstraw,
sea holly, milkwort.
Nobody there but us.
We stayed on — the pale sand, the evening,
the islands all turning
smoke-blue and floating away —
stayed as we'd done so often before,
but might not again,
the times being frailer,
everything being frailer.
Old ways fall away,
the cormorant's wings beat
black on the water,
the world's going spinning off
to God-knows-where.

Earthen

for Andrew and Tina Kavanagh

Sometimes when the sky clears
to a thin astonishing blue
the heart turns, looks over its shoulder
at shadows of the tall perennials
cross-hatching an old brick path.
Wind rises.
Dry seed-heads rattle and bow
like old thoughts.
The rivets on a wooden bench
are rusting. Weeds thrive
in cracked and broken bricks
set far below
the clean high sky.
Yet there is beauty
in such fecklessness, such disrepair.
It is our body's native language.

Unrest

Oh, heart,
why not content yourself
with this beautiful life here on earth?

Why not move through our rooms
like a woman at dusk
and spread a white cloth on our table?

Old

The flung cries of the choughs,
rags on the windy mountain,
the rattling flight of the magpie,
the heron's flop-winged lift.

And the lambs clamouring the morning,
and the tide rushing the harbour,
and the glamour of hunting kestrel
quartering boggy ground.

from *The Red Window*

when consolation returns

it plods in the suck of the mud
where the stubborn-haunched cattle
stumble and slide
through the stones of the broken fields

it sits on the green wooden chair
that the dutchman had carried outside
and set down facing the sea
in that hour when the morning still shone —

it blows in the low salt-rain
and seeps in fine drops
from the strands of lank wool
that have snarled on the barbs of the fence

La Vie en Rose

A lame bike is clamped
to a chain's looping sag
like an old dog nobody wants.

It is missing a wheel.
In the shadows indifferent drinkers
are stretched on the pavement and steps.

It is Sunday, and freezing.
Above them, the roofs
of the church of Saint-Étienne

climb the black sky.
Its stained, weary bells
strike forth a vast, hollow sound.

Osip Mandelstam

Swimming. It's best in the evening.
Best when the fish rise from the depths.

How he could write, it was easy, like swimming.
Once he knew how he couldn't *un*-know.
He took words like 'mother' and 'shadow' and 'linen',
wrote long lines of memory and sorrow and silence,
of violins, young wives (her arms, her white thighs),
of roosters and oxen and stairwells and dresses,
of prisons and black earth and salt-frost and bread,
and far, far away in the depths of the forest
the faint fading hum of Persephone's bees.

Swimming. It's best in the evening.
Best when the day's past, all's lost,
only night lies ahead.

Coming of Age in the Musée d'Orsay

for Mick O'Dea

There's that Cassatt painting I once liked,
a young girl sewing in the summer's green,
her high-necked dress, thinned by the light,
those salmon-pink geraniums, her white skirts.

I pass her by — too wholesome, docile —
or maybe it was all the time I spent
in that strange German book he lent me.
Dix and Beckmann. The black Weimar glitter.

The book   on my bed   all night.

Genesis

If I had it to tell there would still be a garden.
There would be apple trees, leaves wet with rain.
But the walls would be whitethorn, porous and birded:
small spills of song, and the flutter of wings.

And always a wheelbarrow parked by a flowerbed.
And always a rain butt, running black silk.

Winter Morning

You are here, in this one station, now.
This is your portion under the sun.

This waking in the morning,
the soiled tatters of dream heaping the bed,
this gathering yourself
in the grey dawn.

Over and over
something emerging. Submerging.
So little is conscious. So much
dispossessed.

Being here, in this one station,
in a world
running off into the future,
off into the past.

And our dark prayers
crying themselves.

from *Kells Priory*

THE GARDENER'S GRUMBLE

It is January.
Ice-shards in hoof prints. The dark way of silence.
Light lying down on the straw-coloured grasses.
We are cold and ill-tempered but dinner is pig's cheek.
In church they are eating the body of God.

February is Brigit's with spring round the corner
and hard on the spring comes the sweet smell of summer,
three o'clock matins, then dawns wild with birdsong,
and I'm in the garden, shape-changed to a blackbird
grubbing about in the body of God.

Rebellion

I am like an elephant: beat me about the head with blows
so that I will not dream of India and gardens.

— Rumi

No blows. I want to dream
of India and gardens. To ignore
the mahout. To set
one great foot after the other. To sway
off into the jungle. To tramp
down to the river and wallow. To spray
shining showers. To live
in joy and pride and disobedience. To lift
my trunk and trumpet the tremendous skies.

Humankind

We carry the trust.
It was not imposed on us,
nor are we heedless.

Sometimes the stillness stands in the woods
and lies on the lake. We move like drowned beings
through clouded waters.

Sometimes we wake to spent leaves
blowing about in the yard. A door bangs.
A woman — vigorous — shakes a rug into the wind.

The red dog shudders and rises and listens.
Uncertain light shines the grasses.
Wealth sits in inner rooms, staring.

These are our days.
Walk them.
Fear nothing.

September Thoughts

after reading Jean Follain

She squats in the matted woods making water
into the moss and the hush, vague with gnats;
stares at the silvery trail of the slug
round the tea-brown, contorted, inedible fungi —
while up in the house they sit waiting and knowing
that this time is always like this —
                                              is always suspended
centuries deep, and will pass — the trees
will open their hands and the shores of the lake
will clot with drowned leaves; the people will dream
and hoard and die and give birth.
Everything will go on going on, she has only
to lie on the floor reading books.
Already the darkness presses the window.

Helplessness

Oh, heart,
why can't you learn
that there is nothing to do in the world except live in it?

Why can't you take its deep gifts —
the birds and the cars in the rain;
lost keys and the broken-hearted?

Samhain

You can feel the dead crowding.
In the fierce, low sun they've kept their distance:
light-fade and they flock like small brown moths
that dart and fall and crawl and rise and settle,
cloaking my shoulders with their soft, drab wings.

The great saints have their high appointed ritual.
This is a congregation of the parish dead,
local to these scattered fields and farms.

Marriage

for Roisin Lonergan

You see, I remember your childhood,

remember walking away
from that house one June night,
late,
the light blue, you children asleep,
and I, turning round, looking back
at the white birds your mother had called,
white birds like magnolia flames,
to float and dream over that house
all through the short summer darkness,
the long winter darkness,
so fierce her resolve
that it summoned this gentleness.

So what is it like now to leave,
to walk through the door and away?

I know that a hundred years on
you'll still sleep in this house
through the summer's short night,
will still open morning eyes to the light,
and a fading drift of white birds —

Thirty Years

These days there is only a silence between us.
All the shoving and pushing, the sound and the fury,
have stilled. I wake in your arms with the silence.
We lie there inside it, not sleeping, not speaking.
Outside, a racket of birdsong, vibrating the air.

Acknowledgements and Notes

Selected Poems draws on five collections edited by Peter Fallon and published by The Gallery Press: *A Furious Place* (1996), *Cry for the Hot Belly* (2000), *The Sky Didn't Fall* (2003), *The Silence Came Close* (2006) and *Only This Room* (2009). Several of these poems have been revised.

page 32 Early in the seventh century St Gobban founded a monastery at Old Loughlin. St Gobban was succeeded by St Laserian who directed the monastery until 639 AD. Later this monastery was destroyed by fire and was replaced in the thirteenth century by the current stone building. Many of the early monasteries were situated beside spring wells which may have been venerated under earlier religious regimes.

Cromwellians: the armies of Oliver Cromwell, who inflicted such sectarian slaughter on the Catholic population that their name is reviled to this day. Many were paid with confiscated land.

Huguenots: French Protestants who settled in Ireland after fleeing savage sectarian persecution.

page 62 The grounds of St Columb's Church of Ireland Cathedral are bounded by the Walls of Derry. Some of the Protestant defenders, killed in the course of the Siege of Derry in 1689, are buried in its graveyard.

Sumnûn ibn Hamza al-Muhibb was a Sufi mystic from Baghdad known for his utterances on ecstatic love. He died sometime after 900 AD.